Mini-Charm Quilts

Mini-Charm Quilts

18 Clever Projects for 2½" Squares

Compiled by **Lissa Alexander**

Martingale®
Create with Confidence

Moda All-Stars
Mini-Charm Quilts:
18 Clever Projects for 2½" Squares
© 2018 by Martingale & Company®

Martingale®
19021 120th Ave. NE, Ste. 102
Bothell, WA 98011-9511 USA
ShopMartingale.com

Printed in China
23 22 21 20 19 18   8 7 6 5 4 3 2 1

Library of Congress Cataloging-in-Publication Data is available upon request.

ISBN: 978-1-60468-923-5

MISSION STATEMENT

We empower makers who use fabric and yarn to make life more enjoyable.

CREDITS

PUBLISHER AND
CHIEF VISIONARY OFFICER
Jennifer Erbe Keltner

CONTENT DIRECTOR
Karen Costello Soltys

DESIGN MANAGER
Adrienne Smitke

MANAGING EDITOR
Tina Cook

PRODUCTION MANAGER
Regina Girard

ACQUISITIONS EDITOR
Karen M. Burns

COVER AND INTERIOR DESIGNER
Kathy Kotomaimoce

TECHNICAL EDITOR
Nancy Mahoney

PHOTOGRAPHER
Brent Kane

COPY EDITOR
Melissa Bryan

ILLUSTRATOR
Christine Erikson

SPECIAL THANKS

Photos for this book were taken at Lori Clark's The FarmHouse Cottage in Snohomish, Washington.

Contents

INTRODUCTION   7

The Projects

    Rickrack Posies   9

    Spare Time   15

    Pinwheels All in a Row   19

    Cross My Heart Pillow   23

    Game Day   29

    Four-Patch Chain   35

    Howdy Doll Quilt and Pillow   41

    Pinwheel Doll Quilt and Pillow   45

    Bayside   49

    Little Steps, Big Fun!   53

    Charming Journal Cover   57

    Merry-Go-Round   61

    Wonky Pinwheel Pillow   65

    Fireworks   71

    Diamond Pincushion   75

    Peppermint Lane   79

    Tulip Time   85

    Hopscotch Table Runner   91

MEET THE CONTRIBUTORS   95

Introduction

It's the little things that matter most. In a "go big or go home" world, it's easy to lose sight of the fact that the little things often make the difference between a good day and a great day. The same might be true for many of us quilters when we look at our fabric collections. There are great quilts and other projects to be made from the tiniest bits of fabrics—2½" mini-charm squares! We challenged 18 Moda All-Star designers to create clever quilts using one, two, or three of these mini-charm packs (each pack has 42 squares) and what follows is their genius at making delightful projects from the smallest of precut squares.

Continuing our tradition of doing good, royalties for this book will be donated to LCC K-9 Comfort Dogs. The group's mission says "A dog is a friend who brings a calming influence, allowing people to open up their hearts and receive help for what is affecting them." Specially trained LCC K-9 Comfort dogs visit disaster locations, community events, and care facilities around the U.S. wearing their "Please Pet Me" vests—offering comfort where words often fail. It's a little thing— the comfort a four-legged friend can bring—that can make a huge impact in the lives of those hurting. Learn more at their website (k9comfort.org) and thank you, because your purchase of this little book will help make a big difference.

~Lissa Alexander

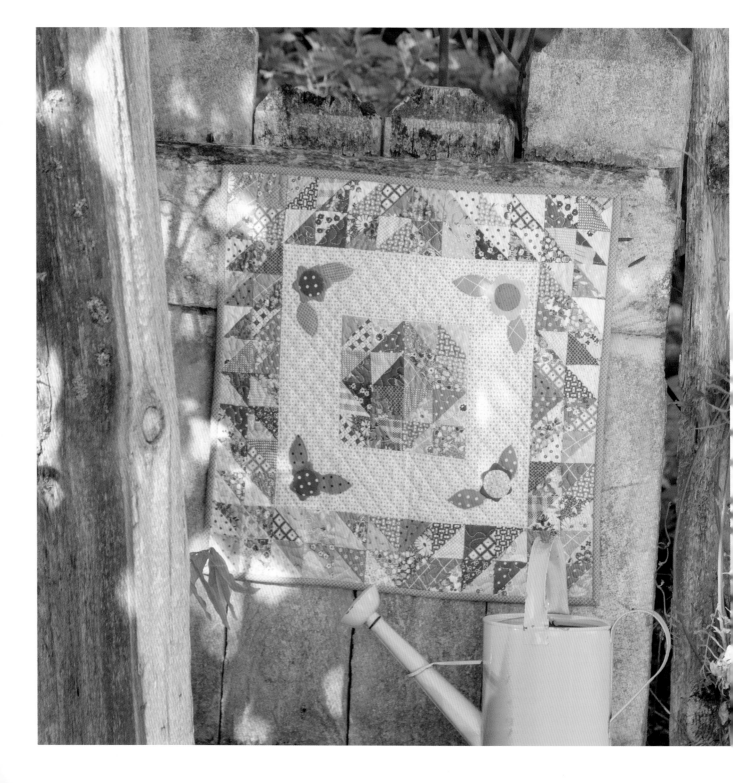

Rickrack Posies by Sandy Klop

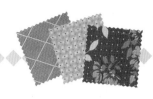

- **FINISHED SIZE: 20" × 20"**
- **FINISHED BLOCK: 3¼" × 3¼"**
- **MINI-CHARM PACKS NEEDED:** ■■■

How does your garden grow? With rickrack flowers, fusible leaves, and half-square triangles all in rows.

Materials

Yardage is based on 42"-wide fabric. Mini-charm squares are 2½" × 2½".

3 mini-charm packs of assorted bright prints for blocks, sorted by:
- 48 light and 48 dark for blocks
- 4 sets of 2 matching green squares for leaves
- 4 bright squares for flower circles

⅓ yard of cream print for inner border
¼ yard of green check for binding
¾ yard of fabric for backing
24" × 24" piece of batting
6" lengths of ½"-wide rickrack in orange, yellow, red, and blue (4 pieces total)
¼ yard of paper-backed fusible web
Cardstock for circle template

Cutting

All measurements include ¼"-wide seam allowances.

From the cream print, cut:
2 strips, 3¾" × 13½"
2 strips, 3¾" × 7"

From the green check, cut:
3 strips, 2¼" × 42"

Works like a charm

from **SANDY KLOP**

Sandy Klop is like the little engine that could when it comes to designing quilts as American Jane (AmericanJane.com). We think she can! We think she can!

If I could invent a new mini-charm pack of something besides fabric, I'd make one out of 2½" squares of mini plants. Maybe then I could manage a garden! But they couldn't grow—they'd have to stay small!

Here's a little something I try to remember when I sit down to sew: Slow down. It's not a race. Take all the time you want.

If I'm not sewing from my own collection of fabrics, the designer group I'd most likely be working with is Minick and Simpson! I love everything they do, and I love Laurie Simpson's sense of humor.

When it comes to basics, I love geometrics—stripes, dots, grids, plaids, letters, numbers, and words.

Lots of good things come in mini size! Besides mini-charm squares, I like mini chairs. I have a great collection, and I have a friend who makes a new one for me every year. I'm so fortunate!

If I had to name a color that every quilt could use a dash of, it'd be yellow or red. No quilt should be without sunshine or at least some passion.

Leftover charms, if there are any, most likely end up in a little suitcase, of course!

Making the Blocks

Separate the mini-charm squares into one group of 48 dark squares and one group of 48 light squares. Press the seam allowances as indicated by the arrows.

1 Draw a diagonal line from corner to corner on the wrong side of each light square. Place a marked square on a dark square, right sides together. Sew ¼" from both sides of the drawn line. Cut on the line to yield two half-square-triangle units. Make 96 units that measure 2⅛" square, including the seam allowances.

Make 96 units,
2⅛" × 2⅛".

2 Lay out four half-square-triangle units in two rows of two units each. Sew the units together in rows. Join the rows to make a block. Make 24 blocks that measure 3¾" square, including the seam allowances.

Make 24 blocks,
3¾" × 3¾".

Assembling the Quilt

1 Lay out four blocks in two rows of two blocks each. Sew the blocks together in rows. Join the rows to make the center section. The section should measure 7" square, including the seam allowances.

Make 1 section,
7" × 7".

2 Sew the cream 3¾" × 7" strips to opposite sides of the center section. Sew the cream 3¾" × 13½" strips to the top and bottom of the section to complete the inner border.

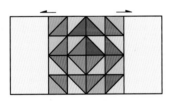

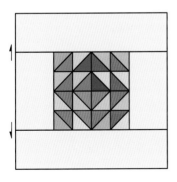

3 Sew four blocks together to make a border unit that measures 3¾" × 13½", including the seam allowances. Make four units.

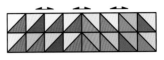

Make 4 units,
3¾" × 13½".

4 Sew border units from step 3 to opposite sides of the quilt top. Sew a block to each end of the remaining two border units. Sew these borders to the top and bottom of the quilt. The quilt top should measure 20" square.

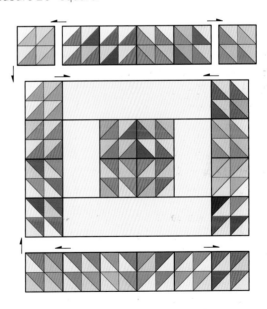

Stitching the Appliqués

For more detailed instructions on fusible appliqué, go to ShopMartingale.com/HowtoQuilt.

1 Using the leaf pattern on page 13, trace eight leaves onto the paper side of the fusible web. Roughly cut out each shape.

2 Following the manufacturer's instructions, press each fusible-web shape onto the wrong side of the green squares. Cut out the leaves on the traced lines.

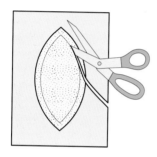

3 Remove the paper backing from each leaf. Referring to the quilt photo on page 9, fuse the leaves onto the cream inner border. Stitch the edges using matching thread and a blanket stitch or narrow zigzag stitch.

4 Make a cardstock circle template using the pattern on page 13. Trace a circle onto the wrong side of each bright print square. Cut out the circles, adding a ⅜" seam allowance around the perimeter.

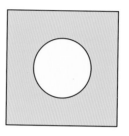 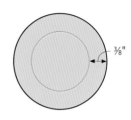

5 Using a needle and thread, hand baste around a traced circle, sewing ¼" from the drawn line. Do not clip the thread. Place the cardstock template in the center of the fabric circle. Pull the thread tails to snugly gather the fabric around the template. Knot the thread. Press well. Snip the basting thread and remove the template. Press again. Repeat to make four gathered circles.

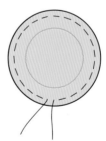 

6 Referring to the quilt photo, position a gathered circle on the cream inner border. Cut the rickrack into four 4½" lengths. Shape one length of rickrack into a curve and place it under the edge of the gathered circle, tucking the ends under the fabric. Pin

the rickrack in place. Remove the fabric circle and stitch through the center of the rickrack to attach the rickrack to the quilt. Reposition the fabric circle on the rickrack. Hand or machine stitch around the edge of the fabric circle. Repeat with each circle.

Finishing the Quilt

For more details on quilting and finishing, go to ShopMartingale.com/HowtoQuilt.

1. Layer the backing, batting, and quilt top; baste the layers together. Hand or machine quilt. The quilt shown is quilted with a diagonal grid in the cream border and a meandering design in the center and the outer border.

2. Using the green 2¼"-wide strips, make the binding and attach it to the quilt.

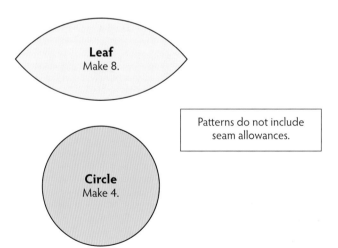

Leaf
Make 8.

Circle
Make 4.

Patterns do not include seam allowances.

Spare Time by Lisa Bongean

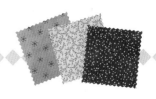

- FINISHED SIZE: 13" × 15½"
- FINISHED BLOCK: 1¼" × 1¼"
- MINI-CHARM PACKS NEEDED: ■■■

Make the most of your sewing time. Tiny Hourglass blocks take just minutes to make when you begin with mini-charm squares.

Materials

Yardage is based on 42"-wide fabric. Mini-charm squares are 2½" × 2½". Fat quarters measure 18" × 21".

3 mini-charm packs of assorted prints for blocks
   (you'll need 60 dark and 60 light squares)
¼ yard of navy print for binding
1 fat quarter of fabric for backing
17" × 20" piece of batting

Cutting

All measurements include ¼"-wide seam allowances.

From the navy print, cut:
2 strips, 2¼" × 42"

STARCHY GOODNESS

To make small pieces like charm squares behave, especially when I'll sew along the bias, I saturate them with spray starch, allow to air dry, and press before cutting or sewing.

Works like a charm

from **LISA BONGEAN**

Lisa Bongean (LisaBongean.com) is a tiny dynamo when it comes to piecing little bitty patchwork from her Primitive Gatherings fabrics.

This tip works like a charm for me every time: Stay organized.

I store my mini-charm packs in a cupboard in my sewing studio.

If I could invent a new mini-charm pack of something besides fabric, I'd make one out of 2½" squares of cheese. I'm from Wisconsin!

Here's a little something I try to remember when I sit down to sew: This is the best part of what we do.

If I'm not sewing from my own collection of fabrics, the designer groups I'd most likely be working with are Betsy Chutchian and Jo Morton.

When it comes to basics, I love Primitive Muslins.

On a day when I can only squeeze in a little time to quilt, I'll most likely spend it stitching.

Lots of good things come in mini size! Besides mini-charm squares, I like mini quilts.

If I'm settled in for sewing and need a good binge-watching show in the background, I'll turn on HGTV or Food Network.

If I had to name a color that every quilt could use a dash of, it'd be all of them. Scrappy is best!

Making the Blocks

Press the seam allowances as indicated by the arrows.

1 Draw a diagonal line from corner to corner on the wrong side of each light square. Place a marked light square on a dark square, right sides together. Sew ¼" from both sides of the drawn line. Cut on the line to yield two half-square-triangle units. Make 120 units that measure 2⅛" square, including the seam allowances.

Make 120 units,
2⅛" × 2⅛".

2 On the wrong side of 60 half-square-triangle units, draw a diagonal line from corner to corner, perpendicular to the seamline. Layer a marked unit on an unmarked unit, right sides together with the dark triangles on top of the light triangles. Sew ¼" from both sides of the drawn line. Cut on the line to yield two Hourglass blocks. Make 120 blocks that measure 1¾" square, including the seam allowances.

Make 120 blocks,
1¾" × 1¾".

Assembling the Quilt

Lay out the blocks in 12 rows of 10 blocks each, rotating the blocks so the dark and light prints alternate. Sew the blocks in each row together. Join the rows to complete the quilt top. The quilt top should measure 13" × 15½".

Quilt assembly

Finishing the Quilt

For more details on quilting and finishing, go to ShopMartingale.com/HowtoQuilt.

1 Layer the backing, batting, and quilt top; baste the layers together. Hand or machine quilt. The quilt shown is quilted with a grid of lines that cross horizontally and vertically through the center of each block.

2 Using the navy 2¼"-wide strips, make the binding and attach it to the quilt.

Pinwheels All in a Row by Jo Morton

- **FINISHED SIZE:** 19" × 26¾"
- **FINISHED BLOCK:** 2½" × 2½"
- **MINI-CHARM PACKS NEEDED:** ■ ■ □

Take a new twist on pinwheels using treasured prints from the past. Align the on-point blocks in vertical rows for a lineup that's sure to please the eye.

Materials

Yardage is based on 42"-wide fabric. Mini-charm squares are 2½" × 2½".

2 mini-charm packs of assorted prints for blocks (you'll need 36 light and 36 dark squares)
⅜ yard of tan print for setting triangles
¾ yard of red check for sashing
¾ yard of red print for border
¼ yard of teal print for binding
¾ yard of fabric for backing
23" × 31" piece of batting

Cutting

All measurements include ¼"-wide seam allowances.

From the tan print, cut:
8 squares, 5" × 5"; cut the squares into quarters diagonally to yield 32 side triangles (2 will be extra)
6 squares, 3" × 3"; cut the squares in half diagonally to yield 12 corner triangles

From the red check, cut on the *lengthwise* grain:
2 strips, 2" × 21¾"

From the red print, cut on the *lengthwise* grain:
2 strips, 3" × 21¾"
2 strips, 3" × 19"

From the teal print, cut:
3 strips, 1⅛" × 42"

Works like a charm

from **JO MORTON**

"If you want to make it all, make it small," has been Jo Morton's (JoMortonQuilts.com) mantra for years. No wonder she's a winner when it comes to sewing with mini-charms.

This tip works like a charm for me every time: Don't be in a hurry cutting or sewing. You'll make fewer mistakes if you keep this in mind.

If I could invent a new mini-charm pack of something besides fabric, I'd make one out of 2½" squares of thread.

If I'm not sewing from my own collection of fabrics, the designer group I'd most likely be working with is Betsy Chutchian.

When it comes to basics, I love prints. I'm not a basics kind of gal.

On a day when I can only squeeze in a little time to quilt, I'll most likely spend it working on whatever is waiting, because I try to leave something waiting just for these moments.

Lots of good things come mini sized! Besides mini-charm squares, I need Dove Miniatures dark chocolate.

If I had to name a color that every quilt could use a dash of, it'd be red.

Leftover charms, if there are any, most likely end up being shared with quilting friends.

Making the Blocks

Divide the mini-charm squares into 18 groups of two different light squares and two contrasting dark squares. Press the seam allowances as indicated by the arrows.

1 Select one group of squares. Draw a diagonal line from corner to corner on the wrong side of the two light squares. Place each marked square on a dark square, right sides together. Sew a scant ¼" from both sides of the drawn lines. Cut on the lines to yield a total of four half-square-triangle units that measure 2⅛" square, including the seam allowances.

Make 2 of each unit,
2⅛" × 2⅛".

2 On the wrong side of two *matching* half-square-triangle units, draw a diagonal line from corner to corner, perpendicular to the seamline. Layer a marked unit on an unmarked unit, right sides together with the dark triangles on top of the light triangles. Sew a scant ¼" from both sides of the drawn line. Cut on the line to yield two hourglass units. Make four hourglass units that measure 1¾" square.

Make 4 units,
1¾" × 1¾".

3 Repeat steps 1 and 2 to make a total of 18 sets of four hourglass units.

4 Arrange one matching set of hourglass units in two rows of two units each, rotating the units so that one of the dark prints forms a pinwheel in the center of the block. Sew the units together in each row. Join the rows to make a block, referring to "Reducing Bulk in Seams" below. Make a total of 18 blocks that measure 3" square, including the seam allowances.

Make 18 blocks,
3" × 3".

REDUCING BULK IN SEAMS

Clip up to the seamline on both sides of the intersection as shown. The clips should be ½" apart and line up with the edges of the seam allowances. Press the seam allowances open to make a flatter intersection.

~Jo

Clip.   Clip.

Assembling the Quilt

1 Lay out six blocks, 10 tan side triangles, and four tan corner triangles in a row with the blocks on point. Sew the setting triangles to the sides of the blocks. Sew the units together; then center and sew the corner triangles to the ends of each row. The setting triangles and corner triangles are cut slightly oversized. Trim and square up the row to measure 4" × 21¾", leaving a ¼" seam allowance beyond the points of the blocks. Make three rows.

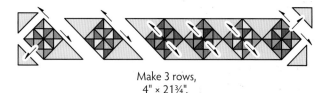

Make 3 rows,
4" × 21¾".

2 Sew the block rows and red check sashing strips together as shown in the quilt assembly diagram on page 22. The quilt top should measure 14" × 21¾", including the seam allowances.

3 Sew the red print 3" × 21¾" strips to opposite sides of the quilt top. Sew the red print 3" × 19"

Single-Fold Binding

1 Sew the binding strips together at a 45° angle as shown and press the seam allowances to one side.

2 Fold over ¼" at one end of the binding strip and press, wrong sides together. Starting with the folded end, position the binding on the quilt, right sides together, and align the edges. Stitch the binding to the quilt top, starting at the center of one side and using a ¼" seam allowance. Stop ¼" from the first corner and backstitch.

3 Remove the quilt from the machine. Turn the quilt and fold the binding straight up, making a 45° angle. Fold the binding back down, aligning it with the edge of the next side. Sew the remaining sides in this way. When you reach the place where you started, stitch over the folded end of the binding; clip the excess.

4 Fold the binding over the raw edges to the back of the quilt. Turn the raw edge under ¼" and slip-stitch to the back of the quilt. Miter the corners as shown.

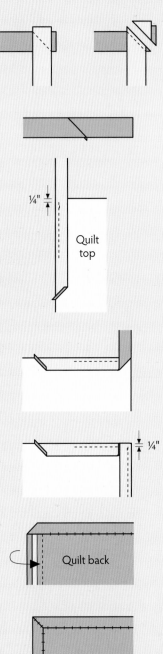

strips to the top and bottom of the quilt. The quilt top should measure 19" × 26¾".

Quilt assembly

Finishing the Quilt

For more details on quilting and finishing, go to ShopMartingale.com/HowtoQuilt.

1 Layer the backing, batting, and quilt top; baste the layers together. Hand or machine quilt. The quilt shown is machine quilted in a diagonal grid.

2 Using the teal 1⅛"-wide strips, make single-fold binding and attach it to the quilt (see "Single-Fold Binding," left).

Cross My Heart Pillow by Brenda Riddle

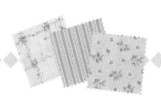

- **FINISHED SIZE: 16½" × 16½"**
- **MINI-CHARM PACKS NEEDED: ■□□**

X marks the spot where you'll fall in love with the clever technique used to create this sweetheart pillow.

Materials

Yardage is based on 42"-wide fabric. Mini-charm squares are 2½" × 2½".

1 mini-charm pack of assorted prints for appliqués (You'll need 15 squares for the pillow top. Use the remaining squares to make the Cross My Heart Quilt on page 27.)

1⅛ yards of tan solid for background, pillow back, and binding

22" × 22" piece of fabric for backing the pillow top

22" × 22" piece of batting

7½" × 12½" piece of paper-backed fusible web

Silicone pressing sheet (optional)

16" × 16" pillow form

Cutting

All measurements include ¼"-wide seam allowances.

From the tan solid, cut:

1 square, 18" × 18"

2 rectangles, 11" × 16½"

2 strips, 2¼" × 42"

Making the Pillow Top

1 Place the fusible web on your ironing surface, fusible side up. Arrange the print squares on the fusible web in five rows of three squares each, placing the squares next to each other so that no fusible shows between them. Press the squares to the fusible web, being careful not to get the fusible on your iron.

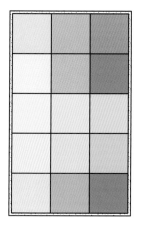

PRESSING FUSIBLE WEB

Cover the rectangle of fusible web and the fabric squares with a silicone pressing sheet to avoid getting sticky residue on your iron.

2 Cut the print squares apart. Trim off the zigzag edges to make 15 squares that measure approximately 2⅜" square.

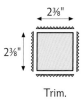

Trim.

3 Cut each print square into quarters horizontally and vertically to make a total of 60 squares, each approximately 1³⁄₁₆" square. Discard five of the small squares or set them aside for another project.

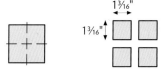

4 Fold each small square in half horizontally and vertically and finger-press to establish center creases. Open a square and mark a dot on the creased line, ¼" from the outer edge on each side. Clip to the dot to remove a tiny triangle from each side of the square as shown. These do not have to be exact! Variety makes the Xs cuter, just like little hand-stitched cross-stitches. Remove the paper backing from the Xs. Make 55.

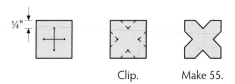

Clip.   Make 55.

Works like a charm

from BRENDA RIDDLE

Brenda Riddle (AcornQuiltandGiftCompany.com) knows that from tiny acorns grow mighty oaks. She also knows that from tiny charm squares come projects to love.

This works like a charm for me every time: Before I start a new project, I pre-wind bobbins and restock pins in the pincushion that sits by my sewing machine. It helps me focus on getting started, and I'm so thankful for them being within reach and ready when I'm in the midst of sewing.

Here's how I store my mini-charm packs: I display all my favorites in a very large glass jar.

If I could invent a new mini-charm pack of something besides fabric, I'd make one out of 2½" squares of scented soaps!

Here's a little something I try to remember when I sit down to sew: Enjoy the process. That way I don't rush, which usually means I then become too familiar with my seam ripper!

If I'm not sewing from my own collection of fabrics, the designer groups I'd most likely be working with are Three Sisters, Blackbird Designs, Tilda, or Liberty Lawn.

On a day when I can only squeeze in a little time to quilt, I'll most likely spend it trimming blocks or hand stitching.

Lots of good things come in mini size! Besides mini-charm squares, I like mini(ature) golf!

5 Fold the tan square in half horizontally and vertically and lightly press to establish centering creases. Mark the center of the square where the creases intersect.

6 Using the creases as a guide and starting in the center, arrange the Xs on the tan square as shown. Following the manufacturer's instructions, fuse the Xs in place.

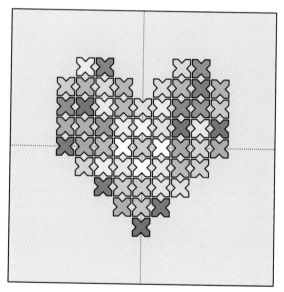

Appliqué placement guide

Finishing the Pillow

For more details on quilting and finishing, go to ShopMartingale.com/HowtoQuilt.

1 Layer the backing, batting, and pillow top; baste the layers together. Hand or machine quilt. The pillow

top shown is quilted with allover meandering that is smaller in the heart than the background to best secure the Xs.

2 Trim the pillow top to 16½" square, keeping the heart design centered.

3 To make the pillow back, fold over ¼" on one 16½" edge of each tan rectangle, toward the wrong side. Fold over ¼" again. Press and stitch close to the folded edges to make a hem.

Make 2.

4 Overlap the pillow backs on top of the pillow top, wrong side together, to make a 16½" square. Pin and machine baste ⅛" from the outer edges.

Baste.

5 Using the tan 2¼"-wide strips, make the binding and attach it to the edges of the pillow. Insert the pillow form through the opening.

Cross My Heart Quilt

You can just as easily make Cross My Heart a quilt!

- **FINISHED SIZE:** 14½" × 14½"
- **MINI-CHARM PACKS NEEDED:** ◼☐☐

Materials

Yardage is based on 42"-wide fabric. Mini-charm squares are 2½" × 2½". Fat quarters measure 18" × 21".

15 mini-charm squares of assorted prints for appliqués

1 fat quarter of white solid for background
¼ yard of blue print for binding
20" × 20" square of fabric for backing
20" × 20" square of batting
7½" × 12½" rectangle of paper-backed fusible web
Silicone pressing sheet (optional)

Cutting

All measurements include ¼"-wide seam allowances.

From the white solid, cut:
1 square, 16" × 16"

From the blue print, cut:
2 strips, 2¼" × 42"

Assembling the Quilt

Assemble the quilt top as for the pillow top on page 25. After quilting, trim to 14½" square, and then bind using the blue print strips.

Game Day by Kathy Schmitz

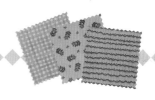

- **FINISHED SIZE:** 28½" × 28½"
- **FINISHED BLOCK:** 8" × 8"
- **MINI-CHARM PACKS NEEDED:** ■ ■ ☐

Add a playful touch to your decor with a table topper inspired by an antique game board. Change the colors to suit your style.

Materials

Yardage is based on 42"-wide fabric. Mini-charm squares are 2½" × 2½".

2 mini-charm packs of assorted green, blue, yellow, and cream prints for blocks, sashing, and borders (you'll need 77 squares total)

1 yard of dark blue print for blocks, sashing, borders, and binding

½ yard of cream print for blocks

⅛ yard *each* of 1 yellow, 1 blue, and 2 green prints for sashing (referred to collectively as "medium prints")

⅛ yard of blue stripe for center block

1 yard of fabric for backing

33" × 33" piece of batting

Cardstock for template

Cutting

All measurements include ¼"-wide seam allowances.

From the cream print, cut:

5 strips, 2½" × 42"; crosscut into:
    16 rectangles, 2½" × 4½"
    36 squares, 2½" × 2½"

Continued on page 30

Continued from page 29

From the dark blue print, cut:

1 strip, 3" × 42"; crosscut into 13 squares, 3" × 3"

6 strips, 2½" × 42"; crosscut into:

    12 rectangles, 2½" × 8½"

    40 squares, 2½" × 2½"

1 strip, 4½" × 42"; crosscut into:

    5 squares, 4½" × 4½"

    3 squares, 3" × 3"

4 strips, 2¼" × 42"

From *each* medium print, cut:

4 rectangles, 2½" × 4½" (16 total)

4 squares, 3" × 3" (16 total)

From the blue stripe, cut:

4 rectangles, 2½" × 4½"

Appliquéing the Circles

1 Make a cardstock circle template using the pattern on page 34. (See "Preparing Appliqué Circles" at right.) Trace the template onto the wrong side of 77 mini-charm squares. Cut out the circles, adding a ⅜" seam allowance around the perimeter.

⅜"

2 Using a needle and thread, hand baste around a traced circle, sewing ¼" from the drawn line. Do not clip the thread. Place the cardstock template in the center of the fabric circle. Pull the thread tails to gather the fabric snugly around the template. Knot the thread. Press well. Snip the basting thread and remove the template. Make 77 circles.

PREPARING APPLIQUÉ CIRCLES

Make 10 to 20 cardstock circle templates so that you can prepare a bunch of circles for appliqué at the same time.

3 Hand stitch a cream circle in the center of each dark blue 4½" square. Make five units.

Make 5 units, 4½" × 4½".

4 Hand stitch a circle in the center of 16 cream and eight dark blue 2½" squares.

Make 16 units, Make 8 units,
2½" × 2½".   2½" × 2½".

5 Place four circles on each dark blue 2½" × 8½" rectangle, spacing them evenly and keeping them ½" from all edges. Hand stitch the circles in place. Make 12 units.

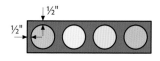

Make 12 units,
2½" × 8½".

Making the Star Blocks

Press the seam allowances as indicated by the arrows.

1 Draw a diagonal line from corner to corner on the wrong side of each remaining cream 2½" square. Place a marked square on opposite corners of an appliquéd dark blue 4½" square as shown. Sew on the drawn lines. Trim the excess corner fabric, ¼" from the stitched line.

2 In the same manner, sew cream squares to the remaining corners of the dark blue square to make a center unit. Make five units that measure 4½" square, including the seam allowances.

Make 5 units,
4½" × 4½".

3 Draw a diagonal line from corner to corner on the wrong side of the remaining dark blue 2½" squares. Place a marked square on one end of a cream 2½" × 4½" rectangle, right sides together. Sew on the drawn line. Trim the excess corner fabric ¼" from the stitched line. Stitch a marked square on the opposite end of the rectangle to make a flying-geese unit. Make 16 units that measure 2½" × 4½", including the seam allowances.

Make 16 units,
2½" × 4½".

4 Lay out one center unit, four flying-geese units, and four appliquéd cream squares in three rows. Sew together the pieces in each row. Join the rows to make a Star block. Make four blocks that measure 8½" square, including the seam allowances.

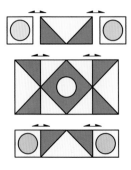 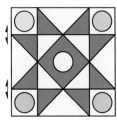

Make 4 blocks,
8½" × 8½".

Making the Center Block

Lay out the remaining center unit, the blue striped rectangles, and four appliquéd dark blue 2½" squares in three rows. Sew together the pieces in each row. Join the rows to make a center block that measures 8½" square, including the seam allowances.

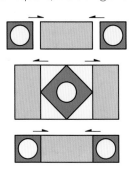 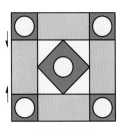

Make 1 block,
8½" × 8½".

Making the Sashing and Borders

1 Draw a diagonal line from corner to corner on the wrong side of each medium print 3" square. Place one marked square on a dark blue 3" square, right sides together. Sew ¼" from both sides of the drawn line. Cut on the line to yield two half-square-triangle units. Trim each unit to measure 2½" square. Make 32 half-square-triangle units.

Make 32 units,
2½" × 2½".

2 Arrange four half-square-triangle units, one of each medium print, as shown. Sew the units together to make a border unit. Make eight units that measure 2½" × 8½", including the seam allowances.

Make 8 units,
2½" × 8½".

3 Join four medium print rectangles, one of each print, as shown. Make four identical units that measure 4½" × 8½", including seam allowances.

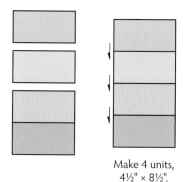

Make 4 units,
4½" × 8½".

4 Sew two appliquéd dark blue rectangles to opposite sides of a unit from step 3 to make a sashing unit. Make four units that measure 8½" square, including the seam allowances.

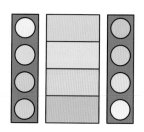 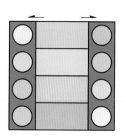

Make 4 units,
8½" × 8½".

Assembling the Quilt

1 Arrange the blocks, sashing units, border units, and remaining appliquéd dark blue rectangles and 2½" squares in five rows as shown below.

2 Sew the pieces in each row together. Join the rows to complete the quilt top. The quilt should measure 28½" square.

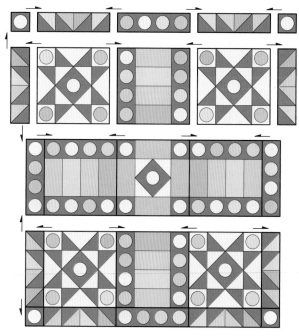

Quilt assembly

Works like a charm

from **KATHY SCHMITZ**

Kathy Schmitz (KathySchmitz.com) is ready to play with mini-charm squares. Put her in, coach!

This tool works like a charm for me every time: a seam ripper . . . ha ha!

I store my mini-charm packs in a large antique glass jar on a shelf in my studio. I love looking at all the colors and textures.

If I could invent a new mini-charm pack of something besides fabric, I'd make one out of 2½" squares of assorted cheeses, crackers, and olive tapenade with three grapes on top.

Here's a little something I try to remember when I sit down to sew: Relax my shoulders and sit up straight.

If I'm not sewing from my own collection of fabrics, the designer group I'd most likely be working with is: Minick and Simpson. They have yummy reds.

When it comes to basics, I love: Crackle! It goes with everything and has a subtly textured background.

On a day when I can only squeeze in a little time to quilt, I'll most likely spend it hand stitching.

Lots of good things come in mini size! Besides mini-charm squares, I love anything mini. I've collected tiny things since I was a girl. I also have Minnie Mouse as my watch face.

If I had to name a color that every quilt could use a dash of, it'd be red.

Finishing the Quilt

For more details on quilting and finishing, go to ShopMartingale.com/HowtoQuilt.

1 Layer the backing, batting, and quilt top; baste the layers together. Hand or machine quilt. The quilt shown is machine quilted around the appliquéd circles, with curved outlines in the half-square-triangle units and rows of circles in the sashing rectangles.

2 Using the dark blue 2¼"-wide strips, make the binding and attach it to the quilt.

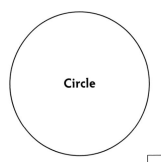

Circle

Pattern does not include seam allowance.

Four-Patch Chain by Barbara Groves and Mary Jacobson

- **FINISHED SIZE:** 28¾" × 28¾"
- **FINISHED BLOCK:** 4" × 4"
- **MINI-CHARM PACKS NEEDED:** ■ ■ □

Pick two cheerful packs of mini-charms and get the party started with a simple four-patch chain set on point.

Materials

Yardage is based on 42"-wide fabric. Mini-charm squares are 2½" × 2½".

2 mini-charm packs of assorted prints for blocks (you'll need 76 squares)

¾ yard of white solid for sashing rectangles and setting triangles

⅓ yard of turquoise print for binding

1 yard of fabric for backing

33" × 33" piece of batting

Cutting

All measurements include ¼"-wide seam allowances.

From the white solid, cut:

5 strips, 2½" × 42"; crosscut into 36 rectangles, 2½" × 4½"

2 squares, 9¾" × 9¾"; cut the squares into quarters diagonally to yield 8 side triangles

2 squares, 6⅝" × 6⅝"; cut the squares in half diagonally to yield 4 corner triangles

From the turquoise print, cut:

4 strips, 2¼" × 42"

Making the Block Rows

Press the seam allowances as indicated by the arrows.

1 Arrange four squares in two rows of two squares each. Sew the squares in each row together. Join the rows to make a Four Patch block. Make 13 blocks that measure 4½" square, including the seam allowances.

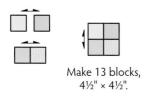

Make 13 blocks,
4½" × 4½".

2 Sew one block and two white rectangles together to make a row. Make two rows that measure 4½" × 8½", including the seam allowances.

Make 2 rows,
4½" × 8½".

3 Sew three blocks and four white rectangles together to make a row. Make two rows that measure 4½" × 20½", including the seam allowances.

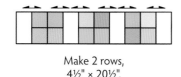

Make 2 rows,
4½" × 20½".

4 Sew five blocks and six white rectangles together to make a row that measures 4½" × 32½", including the seam allowances.

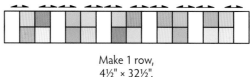

Make 1 row,
4½" × 32½".

Making the Sashing Rows

1 Sew a square to each end of a white rectangle to make a row. Make two rows that measure 2½" × 8½", including the seam allowances.

Make 2 rows,
2½" × 8½".

2 Sew four squares and three white rectangles together to make a row. Make two rows that measure 2½" × 20½", including the seam allowances.

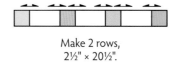

Make 2 rows,
2½" × 20½".

3 Sew six squares and five white rectangles together to make a row. Make two rows that measure 2½" × 32½", including the seam allowances.

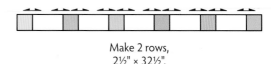

Make 2 rows,
2½" × 32½".

Works like a charm

from **BARBARA GROVES AND MARY JACOBSON**

Barbara Groves and Mary Jacobson are as sweet a pair of sisters as the candy-colored fabric confections they create for their Me and My Sister Designs (MeandMySisterDesigns.com) fabric collections.

This tip works like a charm for us every time: Treat yourself to a new rotary-cutter blade often.

Barb stores her mini-charm packs in an old brown Moda box. Pretty snazzy, right?

If we could invent a new mini-charm pack of something besides fabric, we'd make one out of 2½" squares of chocolate.

Here's a little something we try to remember when we sit down to sew: It's not a race!

If not sewing from our own collection of fabrics, the designer group Barb would most likely be working with is Sweetwater.

When it comes to basics, we love Grunge (by BasicGrey).

On a day when we can only squeeze in a little time to quilt, we'll most likely spend it machine piecing.

Lots of good things come in mini size! Besides mini-charm squares, we like mini dogs.

If she's settled in for sewing and needs a good binge-watching show in the background, Barb says she'll turn on *Pitch Perfect*.

If we had to name a color that every quilt could use a dash of, it'd be green.

Leftover charms, if there are any, most likely end up in the trash.

Assembling the Quilt

1 Join a sashing row to the top of each same-length block row. Make the number of rows indicated.

Make 2 rows,
6½" × 8½".

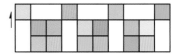

Make 2 rows,
6½" × 20½".

2 For the longest block row, sew a sashing row to the top and bottom.

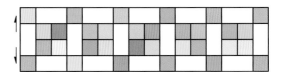

Make 1 row,
8½" × 32½".

3 Lay out the rows from steps 1 and 2 and the white side and corner triangles as shown in the quilt assembly diagram on page 39. Sew the rows and side triangles

together. Join the rows, adding the corner triangles last. The quilt top should measure 28¾" square.

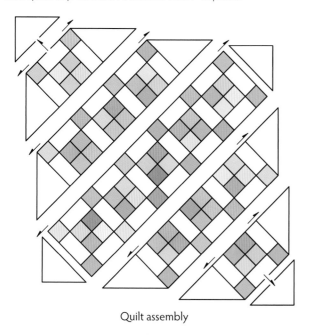

Quilt assembly

Finishing the Quilt

For more details on quilting and finishing, go to ShopMartingale.com/HowtoQuilt.

1 Layer the backing, batting, and quilt top; baste the layers together. Hand or machine quilt. The quilt shown is machine quilted with hearts in the white sashing and setting triangles and a swirl pattern in the print squares.

2 Using the turquoise 2¼"-wide strips, make the binding and attach it to the quilt.

Howdy Doll Quilt and Pillow by Stacey Iest Hsu

- FINISHED QUILT SIZE: 16½" × 16½"
- FINISHED PILLOW SIZE: 6" × 8"
- MINI-CHARM PACKS NEEDED: ■□□

Giddyap and get quilting! Little buckaroos will have a storybook ending to everyday fun with this doll quilt and matching pillow. (The doll and horse are available on the Howdy fabric panel.)

Materials

Yardage is based on 42"-wide fabric. Mini-charm squares are 2½" × 2½". Materials listed are for making both the quilt and the pillow.

1 mini-charm pack of assorted prints for blocks (you'll need 42 squares for the quilt and pillow)
⅓ yard of cream solid for blocks and inner border
¼ yard of blue gingham for outer border
¼ yard of brown gingham for quilt binding
⅔ yard of fabric for backing
21" × 21" piece of batting for quilt
8" × 10" piece of batting for pillow
Polyester fiberfill for pillow

Cutting

All measurements include ¼"-wide seam allowances. Cutting instructions are for the quilt and pillow.

From the cream solid, cut:
4 strips, 1½" × 42"; crosscut into 84 squares, 1½" × 1½"
2 strips, 1" × 42"; crosscut into:
   2 strips, 1" × 13½" (quilt)
   2 strips, 1" × 12½" (quilt)
   2 strips, 1" × 7½" (pillow)
   2 strips, 1" × 4½" (pillow)

Continued on page 42

Continued from page 41

From the blue gingham, cut:

2 strips, 2" × 42"; crosscut into:
 2 strips, 2" × 16½" (quilt)
 2 strips, 2" × 13½" (quilt)
1 strip, 1" × 42"; crosscut into:
 2 strips, 1" × 8½" (pillow)
 2 strips, 1" × 5½" (pillow)

From the brown gingham, cut:

2 strips, 2¼" × 42" (quilt)

From the backing fabric, cut:

1 square, 21" × 21" (quilt)
2 rectangles, 8" × 10" (pillow)

Making the Blocks

Instructions are for making both the quilt and the pillow. Press the seam allowances as indicated by the arrows.

1 Draw a diagonal line from corner to corner on the wrong side of each cream square. Place a marked square on one corner of a print square, right sides together. Sew on the drawn line. Trim the excess corner fabric, ¼" from the stitched line.

2 In the same way, stitch a cream square to the opposite corner of the print square to make a unit. Make 42 units that measure 2½" square, including the seam allowances.

Make 42 units,
2½" × 2½".

3 Join four units in two rows as shown to make a block. Make nine blocks that measure 4½" square, including the seam allowances. Set aside the remaining six units for the pillow.

Make 9 blocks,
4½" × 4½".

Assembling the Quilt

1 Lay out the blocks as shown. Sew the blocks in each row together. Join the rows to complete the quilt-top center, which should measure 12½" square, including the seam allowances.

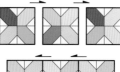

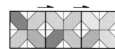
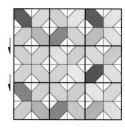

Quilt assembly

2 Sew the cream 1" × 12½" strips to opposite sides of the quilt top. Sew the cream 1" × 13½" strips to the top and bottom. The quilt top should measure 13½" square, including the seam allowances.

3 Sew the blue gingham 2" × 13½" strips to opposites sides of the quilt top. Sew the blue gingham 2" × 16½" strips to the top and bottom. The quilt top should measure 16½" square.

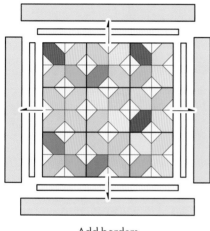

Add borders

Finishing the Quilt

For more details on quilting and finishing, go to ShopMartingale.com/HowtoQuilt.

1 Layer the backing, batting, and quilt top; baste the layers together. Hand or machine quilt. The quilt shown is machine quilted in the ditch.

2 Using the brown gingham 2¼"-wide strips, make the binding and attach it to the quilt.

Making the Pillow

1 Arrange the six remaining units from step 3 of "Making the Blocks" in two rows of three units each. Sew together the units in each row. Join the rows to make the pillow-top center, which should measure 4½" × 6½", including the seam allowances.

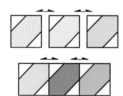 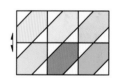

Pillow assembly

2 Sew the cream 1" × 4½" strips to the short ends of the pillow top. Sew the cream 1" × 7½" strips to the long edges of the pillow top. The pillow top should measure 5½" × 7½", including the seam allowances.

Works like a charm

from **STACEY IEST HSU**

Wanna play with mini-charms? No one has more fun imagining the fun you can have than designer Stacy Iest Hsu.

This tip works like a charm for me every time: Clip the corners and curves of my cut-and-sew dolls to remove bulk and create ease. When you turn the doll right side out, the curves will be nice and smooth.

I store my mini-charm packs in a nice stack with all of my other precuts.

If I could invent a new mini-charm pack of something besides fabric, I'd make one out of 2½" squares of fresh mozzarella, tomato, and basil.

Here's a little something I try to remember when I sit down to sew: Don't get caught up in everything being perfect. Purchased quilts or dolls aren't perfect.

If I'm not sewing from my own collection of fabrics, the designer group I'd most likely be working with is Annie Brady.

When it comes to basics, I love Bella Solids.

On a day when I can only squeeze in a little time to quilt, I'll most likely spend it trimming blocks in my car while I wait for my kids to get out of school.

Lots of good things come in mini size! Besides mini-charm squares, I like mini Hagen-Renaker ceramic animal figurines. I give them to my kids for Valentine's Day every year.

If I had to name a color that every quilt could use a dash of, it'd be green.

3 Sew the blue gingham 1" × 5½" strips to the short ends of the pillow top. Sew the blue gingham 1" × 8½" strips to the long edges of the pillow top. The pillow top should measure 6½" × 8½".

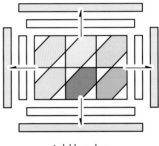

Add borders

4 Layer the backing, batting, and pillow top; baste the layers together. Hand or machine quilt. The pillow shown is machine quilted in the ditch.

5 Layer the pillow top and pillow back rectangle, right sides together. Sew the layers together, leaving a 3" opening in the bottom seam for turning.

6 Turn the pillow right side out. Stuff with polyester fiberfill and hand stitch the opening closed.

Pinwheel Doll Quilt and Pillow
by Stacey Iest Hsu

- FINISHED QUILT SIZE: 14½" × 14½"
- FINISHED PILLOW SIZE: 5" × 8"
- MINI-CHARM PACKS NEEDED: ■□□

Hop along to your sewing machine and stitch a pretty pinwheel doll quilt and pillow to "pardner" with the Howdy Doll Quilt and Pillow on page 41.

Materials

Yardage is based on 42"-wide fabric. Mini-charm squares are 2½" × 2½". Materials listed are for making both the quilt and the pillow.

1 mini-charm pack of assorted prints for blocks*
⅜ yard of cream solid for blocks and border
¼ yard of aqua print for quilt binding
⅝ yard of fabric for backing
19" × 19" piece of batting for quilt
7" × 10" piece of batting for pillow
Polyester fiberfill for pillow

*The quilt and pillow shown require 36 squares.

Cutting

All measurements include ¼"-wide seam allowances. Cutting instructions are for the quilt and pillow.

From the cream solid, cut:
3 strips, 2½" × 42"; crosscut into 36 squares, 2½" × 2½"
2 strips, 1½" × 42"; crosscut into:
    2 strips, 1½" × 14½" (quilt)
    2 strips, 1½" × 12½" (quilt)
    2 strips, 1½" × 8½" (pillow)
    2 strips, 1½" × 3½" (pillow)

Continued on page 46

Continued from page 45

From the aqua print, cut:
2 strips, 2¼" × 42" (quilt)

From the backing fabric, cut:
1 square, 19" × 19" (quilt)
2 rectangles, 7" × 10" (pillow)

Making the Blocks

Press the seam allowances as indicated by the arrows. Instructions are for making both the quilt and pillow.

1 Draw a diagonal line from corner to corner on the wrong side of each cream square. Place a marked square on a print square, right sides together. Sew ¼" from both sides of the drawn line. Cut on the line to yield two half-square-triangle units. Trim the units to 2" square. Make 72.

Make 72 units,
2" × 2".

2 Lay out two pairs of matching half-square-triangle units in two rows as shown. Sew the units in each row together. Join the rows to make a Pinwheel block. Make 18 blocks that measure 3½" square, including the seam allowances.

Make 18 blocks,
3½" × 3½".

Assembling the Quilt

1 Lay out the blocks in four rows of four blocks each as shown in the quilt assembly diagram below. Sew together the blocks in each row. Join the rows to complete the quilt-top center, which should measure 12½" square, including the seam allowances. Set aside the remaining two blocks for the pillow.

2 Sew the cream 1½" × 12½" strips to opposite sides of the quilt top. Sew the cream 1½" × 14½" strips to the top and bottom of the quilt top. The quilt top should measure 14½" square.

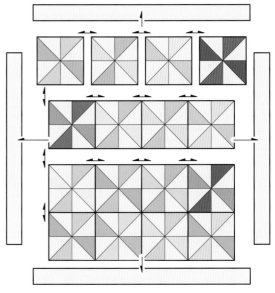

Quilt assembly

3 Finish the quilt as for the Howdy Doll Quilt on page 43.

Making the Pillow

1 Join the two remaining blocks to make the pillow center measuring 3½" × 6½", including seam allowances. Sew the cream 1½" × 3½" strips to the short ends. Sew the cream 1½" × 8½" strips to the long edges. The pillow top should measure 5½" × 8½".

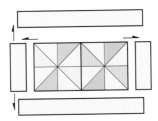

Pillow-top assembly

2 Finish as for the pillow on page 44.

The doll and horse are available on the Howdy fabric panel.

Bayside by Betsy Chutchian

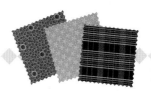

- FINISHED SIZE: 24½" × 33½"
- FINISHED BLOCK: 9" × 9"
- MINI-CHARM PACKS NEEDED: ■■■

Scrappy triangles crisscrossing a field of green belie a simple secret. The quilt is composed of just six straight-set blocks.

Materials

Yardage is based on 42"-wide fabric. Mini-charm squares are 2½" × 2½".

3 mini-charm packs of assorted prints for blocks (you'll need 60 darks and 60 lights)*
¾ yard of green print for blocks and outer border
½ yard of pink print for inner border and binding
⅞ yard of fabric for backing
29" × 38" piece of batting

Medium values can be used as lights or darks, depending on the fabrics they're paired with.

Cutting

All measurements include ¼"-wide seam allowances.

From the green print, cut:
3 strips, 3⅞" × 42", crosscut into 24 squares, 3⅞" × 3⅞". Cut the squares in half diagonally to yield 48 triangles.
2 strips, 2½" × 29½"
2 strips, 2½" × 24½"

From the pink print, cut:
4 strips, 2¼" × 42"
2 strips, 1½" × 27½"
2 strips, 1½" × 20½"

Making the Blocks

Press the seam allowances as indicated by the arrows.

1. Layer a light square on top of a dark square, right sides together. Draw a diagonal line from corner to corner on the light square. Sew ¼" from both sides of the drawn line. Cut on the line to yield two half-square-triangle units. Trim the units to measure 2" square. Make 72 half-square-triangle units.

Make 72 units,
2" × 2".

2. Layer two of the remaining print squares and trim them to 2⅜" square. Cut the layered squares in half diagonally to make two half-square triangles. Cut to make a total of 48 light and 48 dark triangles.

3. Lay out three half-square-triangle units, two dark triangles, and two light triangles as shown. Sew the pieces together into rows. Join the rows to make a center unit. Make 24 units. Sew a green triangle to each side of the center unit to make 24 block quadrants that measure 5" square, including the seam allowances.

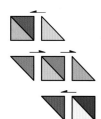

Make 24. Make 24 units,
5" × 5".

4. Arrange four quadrants as shown. Sew them together in rows. Join the rows to make a block. Make six blocks that measure 9½" square, including the seam allowances.

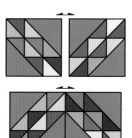 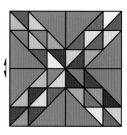

Make 6 blocks,
9½" × 9½".

Assembling the Quilt

1. Arrange the blocks in two vertical rows of three blocks each as shown in the quilt assembly diagram on page 51. Join the blocks in each row; then join the rows to complete the quilt-top center, which should measure 18½" × 27½", including the seam allowances.

2. Sew the pink 1½" × 27½" strips to opposite sides of the quilt center. Sew the pink 1½" × 20½" strips to the top and bottom. The quilt should measure 20½" × 29½", including the seam allowances.

3 Sew the green 2½" × 29½" strips to opposite sides of the quilt center. Sew the green 2½" × 24½" strips to the top and bottom of the quilt. The quilt should measure 24½" × 33½".

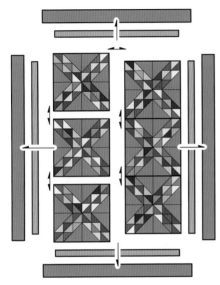

Quilt assembly

Finishing the Quilt

For more details on quilting and finishing, go to ShopMartingale.com/HowtoQuilt.

1 Layer the backing, batting, and quilt top; baste the layers together. Hand or machine quilt. The quilt shown was machine quilted by Sheri Mecom and features feather motifs.

2 Using the pink 2¼"-wide strips, make the binding and attach it to the quilt.

Works like a charm
from BETSY CHUTCHIAN

No doubt about it, she's scrappy! That's why mini-charm packs make the perfect starting point for scrappy quilts in designer Betsy Chutchian's world (BetsysBestQuiltsandMore.blogspot.com).

This tool works like a charm for me every time: Bloc Loc rulers, especially for making half-square triangles.

If I could invent a new mini-charm pack of something besides fabric, I'd make one out of 2½" squares of assorted cheeses and crackers.

Here's a little something I try to remember when I sit down to sew: Trim threads and dog-ears as I sew, and put the trimmings in the trash, not on the floor. And don't sit too long; get up to press often.

If I'm not using my own collection of fabrics, the designer group I'd most likely be working with is Howard Marcus Collection for a Cause.

On a day when I can only squeeze in a little time to quilt, I'll most likely spend it selecting fabrics.

Lots of good things come in mini size! Besides mini-charm squares, I like mini chocolate chips, Cheez-Its, Mini Oreos, and mini patchwork blocks.

If I'm settled in for sewing and need a good binge-watching show in the background, I'll turn on: almost anything on Netflix with lots of dialogue, such as *Gilmore Girls*, *House of Cards*, or *Mad Men*.

If I had to name a color that every quilt could use a dash of, it'd be blue: Prussian, Lancaster, or indigo.

51

Little Steps, Big Fun! by Lynne Hagmeier

- **FINISHED SIZE: 18½" × 18½"**
- **FINISHED BLOCK: 2" × 2"**
- **MINI-CHARM PACKS NEEDED:** ■■□

Build a staircase block-by-block with ease. An easy-to-learn layered-patchwork technique makes assembly a breeze and perfect points a snap to achieve.

Materials

Yardage is based on 42"-wide fabric. Mini-charm squares are 2½" × 2½".

2 mini-charm packs of assorted prints for blocks
    (you'll need 49 dark and 13 tan squares)
½ yard of red print for border and binding
¾ yard of fabric for backing
23" × 23" piece of batting
Fabric glue stick

Cutting

All measurements include ¼"-wide seam allowances.

From the red print, cut:
2 strips, 2½" × 42"; crosscut into:
    2 strips, 2½" × 18½"
    2 strips, 2½" × 14½"
3 strips, 2¼" × 42"

Works like a charm

from **LYNNE HAGMEIER**

Lynne Hagmeier of Kansas Troubles Quilters (KTQuilts.com) is a smooth operator when it comes to layering on the (mini) charm(s). But she's willing to share all the secrets to her successful method.

This tip works like a charm for me every time: Use consistent ¼" seam allowances.

I store my mini-charm packs in vintage anything—tins, wooden boxes, and jars. If a mini-charm pack fits in it, it's an authorized purchase.

If I could invent a new mini-charm pack of something besides fabric, I'd make one out of 2½" squares of Meyer lemon cookies.

If I'm not sewing from my own fabric collection, the designer group I'd most likely be working with is Me and My Sister Designs or Janet Clare.

When it comes to basics, I love Grunge by BasicGrey.

On a day when I can only squeeze in a little time to quilt, I'll most likely spend it making a test block.

Lots of good things come in mini size! Besides mini-charm squares, I like mini chocolate chips. I sprinkle them into my yogurt.

If I'm settled in for sewing and need a good binge-watching show in the background, I'll turn on reruns of *Law & Order: SVU.*

If I had to name a color that every quilt could use a dash of, it'd be red.

Making the Blocks

Press the seam allowances as indicated by the arrows.

1 Cut each tan square into quarters horizontally and vertically to make a total of 52 small squares. *Do not* trim off the pinked edges. You'll need 49 squares; three will be extra.

Cut.

2 Place a tan square on one corner of a dark 2½" square, *right sides up,* aligning the cut edges of the tan square with the edges of the dark square. Use a fabric glue stick to hold the tan square in place. Topstitch ⅛" from the pinked edges of the tan square (these edges will remain raw). Make 49 blocks that measure 2½" square, including the seam allowances.

Make 49 blocks,
2½" × 2½".

Assembling the Quilt

1 Arrange the blocks in seven rows of seven blocks each as shown in the quilt assembly diagram on page 55. Sew the blocks together in each row. Join the rows to complete the quilt-top center, which should measure 14½" square, including the seam allowances.

2 Sew the red 2½" × 14½" strips to opposite sides of the quilt top. Sew the red 2½" × 18½" strips to the top and bottom of the quilt to complete the border. The quilt top should measure 18½" square.

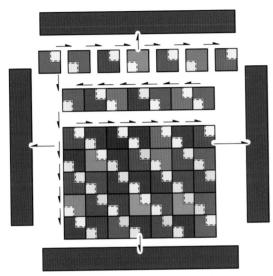

Quilt assembly

Finishing the Quilt

For more details on quilting and finishing, go to ShopMartingale.com/HowtoQuilt.

1 Layer the backing, batting, and quilt top; baste the layers together. Hand or machine quilt. The quilt shown was machine quilted by Joy Johnson with diagonal lines through the blocks and parallel lines across the borders.

2 Using the remaining red 2¼"-wide strips, make the binding and attach it to the quilt.

Charming Journal Cover by Corey Yoder

- FINISHED SIZE: 8" × 10¾" (closed), 16½" × 10¾" (open)
- FINISHED BLOCK: 1½" × 1½"
- MINI-CHARM PACKS NEEDED: ▪ ▪ ▪

Jot this down! Quilters and fabric lovers alike will take note of the scrappy goodness this distinctive cover gives an ordinary notebook.

Materials

Yardage is based on 42"-wide fabric. Mini-charm squares are 2½" × 2½". Fat quarters measure 18" × 21".

3 mini-charm packs of assorted prints for blocks
   (you'll need 102 squares)
⅓ yard of gray solid for blocks
⅜ yard of aqua print for pockets
¼ yard of gray print for binding
1 fat quarter of fabric for backing
17" × 21" piece of batting
7½" × 9¾" composition notebook

Cutting

All measurements include ¼"-wide seam allowances.

From the gray solid, cut:
7 strips, 1¼" × 42"; crosscut into 204 squares,
   1¼" × 1¼"

From the aqua print, cut:
1 strip, 10¾" × 42"; crosscut into:
   2 rectangles, 9½" × 10¾"
   2 rectangles, 3½" × 10¾"

From the gray print, cut:
2 strips, 2¼" × 42"

Making the Journal Cover

Press the seam allowances as indicated by the arrows.

1 Cut the print squares in half to make 204 rectangles that measure 1¼" × 2½".

Cut.

2 Join two rectangles of different prints to make a pieced unit. Make 102 units; trim to 2" square.

Make 102 units,
2" × 2".

3 Draw a diagonal line from corner to corner on the wrong side of each gray 1¼" square. Position a pieced unit with the seam horizontal. Place marked squares on opposite corners of the unit as shown, right sides together. Sew on the drawn lines. Trim the excess corner fabric ¼" from the stitched lines. Make 102 blocks measuring 2" square, including the seam allowances.

Make 102 blocks,
2" × 2".

4 Lay out the blocks in eight rows of 11 blocks each, rotating every other block as shown. Join the blocks in each row. Join the rows to make a pieced rectangle that measures 12½" × 17".

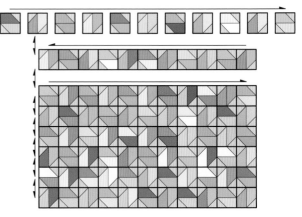

Quilt assembly

5 Layer the backing, batting, and patchwork; baste the layers together. Hand or machine quilt. The project shown is machine quilted with an allover loopy design. Trim the piece to 10¾" × 16½".

6 Join seven blocks as shown to make a row. Trim an equal amount from each end so that the row measures 2" × 10¾". Make two rows.

Make 2 rows,
2" × 10¾".

7 Sew an aqua 3½" × 10¾" strip to one edge of each row from step 6. Sew an aqua 9½" × 10¾" rectangle to the opposite long edge of each row. Make two units that measure 10¾" × 14". Fold each unit in half and press to make two pockets that measure 7" × 10¾".

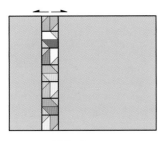 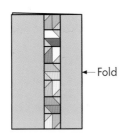

← Fold

Make 2 units,
10¾" × 14".

Make 2 pockets,
7" × 10¾".

Finishing the Journal Cover

1 Layer the quilted rectangle and the pockets, wrong sides together, aligning the outer raw edges. The folded edge of each pocket should be toward the center. Baste the pockets to the cover around the outer edges.

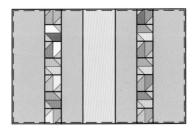

Baste.

2 Using the gray 2¼"-wide strips, make the binding and attach it to the journal cover. Insert the composition book covers into the pockets.

Works like a charm

from COREY YODER

Quilters love Corey Yoder (CorianderQuilts.com) because her fabrics and patterns are cute-as-can-be!

This tool works like a charm for me every time: my Clover thread-cutter pendant. I love it for snipping threads when I'm chain piecing.

I store my mini-charm packs in a cookie jar!

If I could invent a new mini-charm pack of something besides fabric, I'd make one out of 2½" squares of sea-salt caramels.

Here's a little something I try to remember when I sit down to sew: turn on the iron *before* I sit down.

If I'm not sewing from my own collection of fabrics, the designer group I'd most likely be working with is Fig Tree, Sherri & Chelsi, or Lella Boutique.

When it comes to basics, I love Mochi Linen and Bella Solids.

On a day when I can only squeeze in a little time to quilt, I'll most likely spend it making blocks.

Lots of good things come in mini size! Besides mini-charm squares, I like mini blocks and quilts.

If I'm settled in for sewing and need a good binge-watching show in the background, I'll turn on a podcast. I always listen while I sew.

If I had to name a color that every quilt could use a dash of, it'd be gray.

Merry-Go-Round by Karla Eisenach

- **FINISHED SIZE:** 20" × 26"
- **FINISHED BLOCK:** 4½" × 4½"
- **MINI-CHARM PACKS NEEDED:** ■■□

Mini-charms go for a different spin, pieced into scrappy hexagons before being appliquéd in place.

Materials

Yardage is based on 42"-wide fabric. Mini-charm squares are 2½" × 2½". Fat eighths measure 9" × 21".

2 mini-charm packs of assorted prints for blocks
(you'll need 72 squares)
⅜ yard of white solid for block backgrounds
⅓ yard of black print for sashing
1 fat eighth of red gingham for cornerstones
¼ yard of red print for binding
¾ yard of fabric for backing
24" × 30" piece of batting

Cutting

All measurements include ¼"-wide seam allowances.

From the white solid, cut:
2 strips, 5" × 42"; crosscut into 12 squares, 5" × 5"

From the black print, cut:
4 strips, 2" × 42"; crosscut into 31 rectangles, 2" × 5"

From the red gingham, cut:
2 strips, 2" × 21"; crosscut into 20 squares, 2" × 2"

From the red print, cut:
3 strips, 2¼" × 42"

Making the Blocks

Press the seam allowances as indicated by the arrows.

1 Mark the center of a print square along the top edge. Using a rotary cutter and ruler, cut from the bottom corners to the mark to make a triangle. Cut a total of 72 triangles. Discard the trimmed pieces.

Cut 72 triangles.

2 Lay out six triangles in two rows as shown. Sew the triangles in each row together. Join the rows to make a hexagon unit. Make 12 hexagon units.

Make 12 units.

3 Press the edges of each hexagon unit ¼" toward the wrong side. Center a unit on a white square. Hand or machine appliqué in place to make a block. Make 12 blocks that measure 5" square, including the seam allowances.

Make 12 blocks,
5" × 5".

Assembling the Quilt

1 Sew four red gingham squares and three black rectangles together to make a sashing row. Make five rows that measure 2" × 20", including the seam allowances.

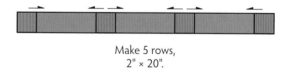

Make 5 rows,
2" × 20".

2 Sew three blocks and four black rectangles together to make a block row. Make four rows that measure 5" × 20", including the seam allowances.

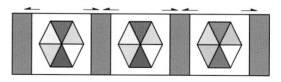

Make 4 rows,
5" × 20".

3 Lay out the sashing rows and block rows as shown in the quilt assembly diagram below. Sew the rows together to make the quilt top. The quilt top should measure 20" × 26".

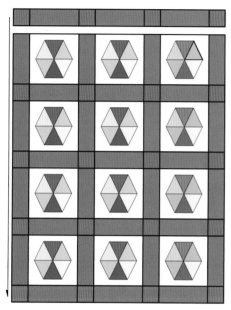

Quilt assembly

Finishing the Quilt

For more details on quilting and finishing, go to ShopMartingale.com/HowtoQuilt.

1 Layer the backing, batting, and quilt top; baste the layers together. Hand or machine quilt. The quilt shown is outline quilted around the hexagons and in each sashing rectangle.

2 Using the red print 2¼"-wide strips, make the binding and attach it to the quilt.

Works like a charm

from KARLA EISENACH

Twist and shout! Karla Eisenach is one third of the fun trio that is Sweetwater (TheSweetwaterCo.com).

If I could invent a new mini-charm pack of something besides fabric, I'd make a 2½"-square Big Mac and call it a Mini Mac.

Here's a little something I try to remember when I sit down to sew: *Try* is the key word—TRY to sew in an uncluttered area.

When it comes to basics, I love Bella solids—in porcelain for sure!

On a day when I can only squeeze in a little time to quilt, I'll most likely spend it hand sewing, appliquéing, or embroidering, because I'm always behind.

Lots of good things come in mini size! Besides mini-charm squares, I like mini candy bars—anything with chocolate.

If I'm settled in for sewing and need a good binge-watching show in the background, I'll turn on *Heartland* on Netflix.

If I had to name a color that every quilt could use a dash of, it'd be black.

Leftover charms, if there are any, most likely end up in a scrap pile.

Wonky Pinwheel Pillow by Brigitte Heitland

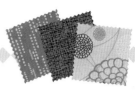

- FINISHED SIZE: 16" × 16"
- FINISHED UNIT: 2" × 2"
- MINI-CHARM PACKS NEEDED: ■ ■ ■

A fun patchwork technique will have you reaching for the stars. Sew, flip, trim, and repeat—no foundation piecing required!

Materials

Yardage is based on 42"-wide fabric. Mini-charm squares are 2½" × 2½".

3 mini-charm packs of assorted prints for patchwork units*
1 yard of blue solid for background and backing
16" × 16" pillow form

The pillow top shown requires 100 squares.

Cutting

All measurements include ¼"-wide seam allowances.

From the blue solid, cut:
4 strips, 2½" × 42"; crosscut into 64 squares, 2½" × 2½"
1 strip, 16½" × 42"; crosscut into 2 rectangles, 16½" × 21"

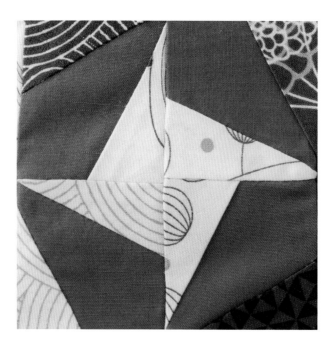

Making the Units

Press the seam allowances as indicated by the arrows.

1 On the wrong side of a blue solid square, mark a dot ¼" down from the top edge and ¼" in from the right edge. Draw two lines through the dot to about the halfway point on the opposite sides of the square as shown.

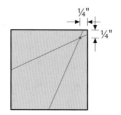

2 Place the marked square on a print square, right sides together, with the top line ¼" *above* the diagonal center of the print square. Sew on the top line.

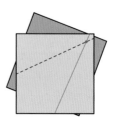

CHECK PLACEMENT OF SQUARES

Before sewing, hold the squares together or pin them together along the line. Fold the print square over the corner of the blue solid square to make sure the print fabric will completely cover the corner of the blue solid square. Adjust the placement if necessary.

3 Fold the print square over the corner along the stitching line. Make sure the corner of the blue solid square is covered; press. Flip the unit over, and trim the print square even with the edges of the blue solid square.

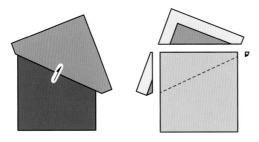

4 Unfold the squares and trim the seam allowance to ¼". Make 64 single-point units that measure 2½" square.

Make 64 units,
2½" × 2½".

5 On 36 of the units from step 4, sew another print square along the remaining marked line. Fold the print square over the corner along the seamline; press. Trim the print square even with the edges of the blue solid square and then trim the seam allowance to ¼". Make 36 double-point units that measure 2½" square, including the seam allowances.

Make 36 units,
2½" × 2½".

EASY ON THOSE SEAMS!

These patchwork units are fun to sew, but once you trim the print pieces, the edges are no longer on the straight of grain. Handle the units carefully. When joining them, pin at the beginning and end of the units and ease the seams in between to keep everything smooth and under control.

Assembling the Pillow Top

1 Arrange the single- and double-point units in eight rows of eight units each as shown in the pillow-top assembly diagram. Make sure the single-point units are all around the outer edges. Double-check to make sure the units are all rotated properly to form the stars.

2 Sew the units in each row together. Join the rows to complete the pillow top.

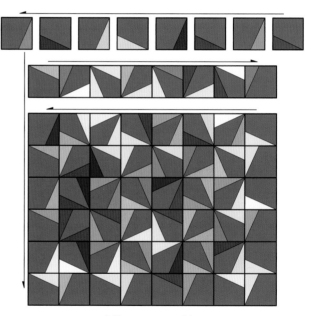

Pillow-top assembly

Finishing the Pillow

1 Fold both blue 16½" × 21" rectangles in half to make two rectangles that are 16½" × 10½"; press. Overlap the folded edges of the two rectangles to create a 16½" backing square; baste the overlapped sections together, stitching ⅛" from the outer edge.

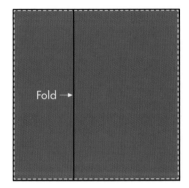

Baste.

2 Layer the backing square and pillow top right sides together. Sew around the perimeter. Clip the corners and turn the pillow right side out and press. Insert the pillow form through the back opening.

Works like a charm

from BRIGITTE HEITLAND

Modern quilter extraordinaire Brigitte Heitland of Zen Chic fame (BrigitteHeitland.de) has stars in her eyes and her mind on design. She'll have you feeling Zen about your patchwork in no time!

This tip works like a charm for me every time: Sew with a *scant* ¼" seam allowance. This way you will always be able to trim the block just a little bit to achieve the perfect size.

I store my mini charm packs in an Ikea transparent plastic box so they're visible. Otherwise, out of sight can mean out of mind.

If I could invent a new mini charm pack of something besides fabric, I'd make one out of 2½" squares of cute illustrated thank-you cards.

Here's a little something I try to remember when I sit down to sew: Imagine you are on vacation/holiday and have all the time you wish to follow your passion.

If I'm not sewing from my own collection of fabrics, the designer group I'd most likely be working with is Sweetwater.

When it comes to basics, I love Bella Solids and low-volume prints.

On a day when I can only squeeze in a little time to quilt, I'll most likely spend it doing hand sewing such as bindings or working on a little English-paper-piecing project.

Lots of good things come in mini size! Besides mini charm squares, I like mini laundry clips for hanging things on my inspiration board.

If I'm settled in for sewing and need a good binge-watching show in the background, I'll turn on an audiobook, because I can fully visually concentrate on sewing while having a good story to listen to.

If I had to name a color that every quilt could use a dash of, it'd be Zen Grey from Bella Solids.

Leftover charms, if there are any, most likely end up in patchwork used to make little pouches.

69

Fireworks by Jen Kingwell

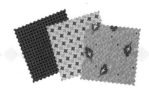

- FINISHED SIZE: 18½" × 18½"
- MINI-CHARM PACKS NEEDED: ■ ■ ■

Draw on your inner artist. A pinch of embroidery, a dash of color, and a background radiating from dark to light equals a sweet and simple quilt.

Materials

Yardage is based on 42"-wide fabric. Mini-charm squares are 2½" × 2½".

2 mini-charm packs of gray prints for background (you'll need 81 squares)
1 mini-charm pack of assorted bright prints for circle appliqués (you'll need 18 squares)
¼ yard of bright stripe for binding
¾ yard of fabric for backing
23" × 23" piece of batting
Assorted bright colors of embroidery floss
Cardstock for templates

Cutting

All measurements include ¼"-wide seam allowances.

From the bright stripe, cut:
3 strips, 2¼" × 42"

Assembling the Quilt

Press the seam allowances as indicated by the arrows.

1 Arrange the gray squares in nine rows of nine squares each as shown. Start with the darkest squares in the center and complete the layout with the lightest squares around the outer edges. Sew together the squares in each row. Join the rows to make a background that measures 18½" square.

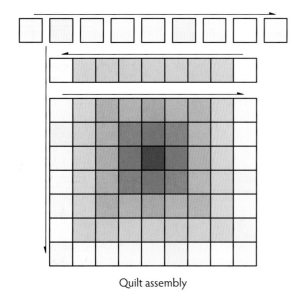

Quilt assembly

2 Use the patterns on page 73 to make an A, a B, and a C circle template from cardstock. On the wrong side of the bright squares, trace seven A circles, four B circles, and seven C circles. Cut out the circles, adding a generous ¼" seam allowance around the perimeter.

3 Using a needle and thread, hand baste around a traced circle, sewing ⅛" from the drawn line. Do not clip the thread. Place a cardstock template in the center of the fabric circle. Pull the thread tails to snugly gather the fabric around the template. Knot the threads. Press well. Snip the basting thread and remove the template. Repeat with each circle.

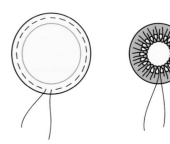

4 Referring to the photo on page 71 for placement ideas, arrange the circles on the quilt top. Hand or machine appliqué them in place.

Finishing the Quilt

For more details on quilting and finishing, go to ShopMartingale.com/HowtoQuilt.

1 Layer the backing, batting, and quilt top; baste the layers together.

2 Referring to the stitch diagrams on page 73, embellish the quilt with running stitches and French knots, using two strands of embroidery floss. Stitch through all layers. The embroidery will serve as quilting stitches.

3 Using the bright striped 2¼"-wide strips, make the binding and attach it to the quilt.

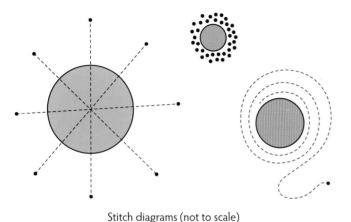

Stitch diagrams (not to scale)

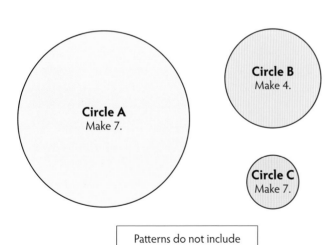

Circle A
Make 7.

Circle B
Make 4.

Circle C
Make 7.

Patterns do not include
seam allowances.

Jen Kingwell (JenKingwellDesigns.blogspot.com) elicits plenty of oohs and aahs over her patchwork and embroidery fireworks show.

This tool works like a charm for me every time: I use a Hera marker to mark hand-quilting lines.

I store my mini-charm packs in a drawer.

If I could invent a new mini-charm pack of something besides fabric, I'd make one out of 2½" squares of brownies.

Here's a little something I try to remember when I sit down to sew: Breathe, especially when machine sewing.

If I'm not sewing from my own collection of fabrics, the designer group I'd most likely be working with is Zen Chic.

When it comes to basics, I love Moda Grunge by BasicGrey.

Lots of good things come in mini size! Besides mini-charm squares, I like mini vacations.

If I'm settled in for sewing and need a good binge-watching show in the background, I'll turn on the Food Channel.

If I had to name a color that every quilt could use a dash of, it'd be chartreuse.

Leftover charms, if there are any, most likely end up as the background for appliqué blocks, just as they did here!

Diamond Pincushion by Laurie Simpson

- **FINISHED SIZE:** 3¾" diameter × 2¼" tall
- **MINI-CHARM PACKS NEEDED:** ■■□

Try your hand at English paper piecing for a patchwork pincushion that's practically perfect in every way.

Materials

Yardage is based on 42"-wide fabric. Mini-charm squares are 2½" × 2½".

2 mini-charm packs of assorted prints for pincushion (you'll need 6 blue, 11 red, 23 cream, and 8 cream-and-red squares)
5" × 5" square of muslin or scrap fabric for bottom lining
5" × 5" piece of batting
Stuffing of choice for pincushion
Cardstock for templates

Making the Pincushion

Press the seam allowances as indicated by the arrows.

1 Arrange four cream-and-red squares in two rows. Sew the squares in each row together. Join the rows to make a four-patch unit. Make two units that measure 4½" square, including the seam allowances.

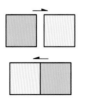

Make 2 units,
4½" × 4½".

5 Place two jewel pieces right sides together. Using tiny hand stitches, slipstitch the pieces together along one short side as shown, catching one or two threads of the fabric with your needle. Do not stitch through the cardstock.

Stitch.

6 Stitch three jewel pieces together to make a half star. Make two half-star units. Sew the hexagon between the half-star units and then stitch the remaining seams to complete the star. Press well. Remove the basting stitches and the cardstock templates.

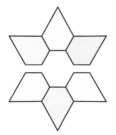 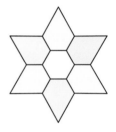

2 For the pincushion bottom, layer the muslin square, batting, and one of the four-patch units. Quilt as desired.

3 Use the patterns on page 78 to make one hexagon, six jewels, 11 diamonds, and 22 half-diamond templates from cardstock.

4 Place a cardstock jewel shape on one blue square. Cut out the shape, leaving ¼" around the template. Center the template on the wrong side of the fabric piece, and fold the seam allowances over the edges of the template. Hand baste around the piece to secure the seam allowances. Prepare six blue jewel pieces, one cream hexagon, 11 red diamonds, and 22 cream half diamonds in this manner.

7 Using the same method, join the red diamonds and cream half diamonds as shown. Stitch the ends together to make a cylinder. Press well. Remove the basting stitches and the cardstock templates.

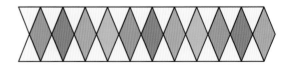

¼"

Baste.

Assembling the Pincushion

1 Center the star on the top four-patch unit and hand baste or pin it in place. Appliqué the star. Use the circle pattern on page 78 to make a cardstock template. Using the template, trace the circle onto the appliquéd unit, keeping the star centered. Cut out the top star unit. Trace the circle onto the quilted bottom unit and cut out the bottom circle.

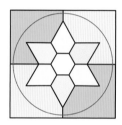 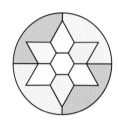

2 Fold the diamond cylinder in quarters and pin-mark each quarter. Sew one side of the cylinder to the top circle, right side together and aligning the marks with the seams on the circle. Sew the other side of the cylinder to the bottom circle, leaving a 1½" opening for turning.

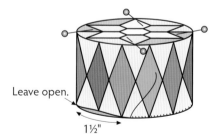

Leave open.

1½"

3 Turn the pincushion right side out through the opening. Fill with the stuffing of your choice. Hand stitch the opening closed.

Works like a charm

from **LAURIE SIMPSON**

Laurie Simpson is half of the Minick and Simpson fabric design duo (MinickandSimpson.blogspot.com). If we had to pin her down, she would choose red over blue—but only by a thread.

This tip works like a charm for me every time: Never use just one fabric when you can use a dozen.

I store my mini-charm packs in a stack on a shelf with other precuts (not too exciting, I know).

If I'm not sewing from my own collection of fabrics, the designer group I'd most likely be working with is American Jane.

When it comes to basics, I love Moda Crossweaves.

On a day when I can only squeeze in a little time to quilt, I'll most likely spend it hand quilting.

If I'm settled in for sewing and need a good binge-watching show in the background, I'll turn on *Agatha Christie's Poirot.* Yes, I have all 13 seasons on DVD.

If I had to name a color that every quilt could use a dash of, it'd be red.

Leftover charms, if there are any, most likely end up in my scrap bin for appliqué.

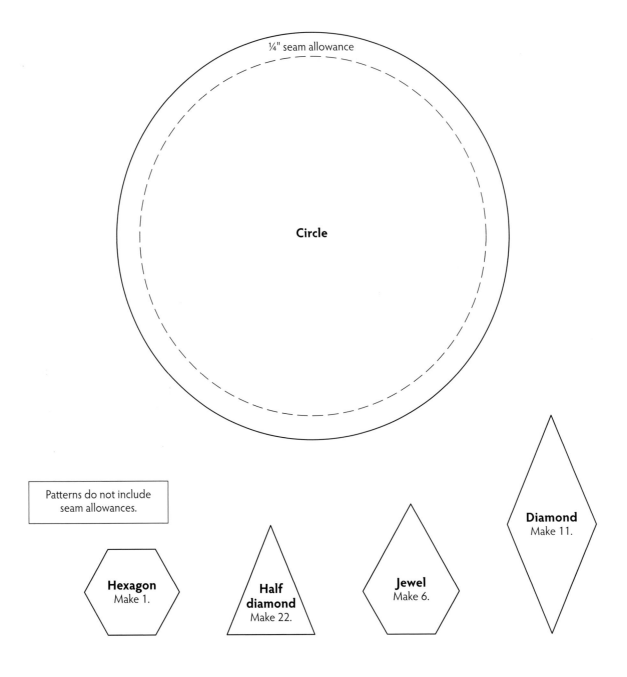

¼" seam allowance

Circle

Patterns do not include
seam allowances.

Hexagon
Make 1.

Half
diamond
Make 22.

Jewel
Make 6.

Diamond
Make 11.

Peppermint Lane by Anne Sutton

Materials

Yardage is based on 42"-wide fabric. Mini-charm squares are 2½" × 2½". Fat quarters measure 18" × 21"; fat eighths measure 9" × 21".

2 mini-charm packs of assorted prints for blocks and appliqués, sorted by:
- 60 assorted prints for blocks
- 4 green for trees
- 2 brown for tree trunks and door
- 1 pink for house
- 1 gray for window

¼ yard of white-on-white print for sashing and border

1 fat eighth of green print for grass

1 fat eighth of gray-on-white print for background

1 fat eighth of red print for cornerstones

¼ yard of red stripe for roof appliqué and binding

1 fat quarter of fabric for backing

20" × 20" piece of batting

- **FINISHED SIZE: 15½" × 16"**
- **FINISHED BLOCK: 2" × 2"**
- **MINI-CHARM PACKS NEEDED: ■■□**

Sugarplum fairies surely live on this tree-lined street. Courthouse Steps blocks form a patchwork of cute-as-can-be cobblestones.

Cutting

All measurements include ¼"-wide seam allowances.

From *each* of 20 assorted print squares, cut:
1 square, 1½" × 1½" (20 total)

From *each* of 20 assorted print squares, cut:
2 rectangles, 1" × 1½" (40 total)

From *each* of 20 assorted print squares, cut:
2 rectangles, 1" × 2½" (40 total)

From the white-on-white print, cut:
2 strips, 1½" × 42"; crosscut into:
    2 strips, 1½" × 14"
    2 strips, 1½" × 13½"
4 strips, 1" × 42"; crosscut into 49 rectangles, 1" × 2½"

From the green print, cut:
1 strip, 1" × 13½"

From the gray-on-white print, cut:
1 strip, 3" × 13½"

From the red print, cut:
2 strips, 1" × 21"; crosscut into 30 squares, 1" × 1"
4 squares, 1½" × 1½"

From the red stripe, cut:
2 strips, 2¼" × 42"

Making the Blocks

Press the seam allowances as indicated by the arrows.

Sew two matching print 1" × 1½" rectangles to opposite sides of a print 1½" square. Sew two matching print 1" × 2½" rectangles to the top and bottom to make a block. Make 20 blocks that measure 2½" square, including the seam allowances.

Make 20 blocks,
2½" × 2½".

Making the Appliquéd Row

For more detailed instructions on appliqué, go to ShopMartingale.com/HowtoQuilt.

1 Using the patterns on page 83 and your preferred appliqué method, make four trees, four tree trunks, one house, one window, and one door from the appropriate color square. Make one roof from the leftover striped fabric.

2 Sew the green strip to the bottom of the gray-on-white strip to make a pieced rectangle that measures 3½" × 13½", including the seam allowances.

3 Referring to the quilt photo on page 80, use matching thread to appliqué the shapes onto the pieced rectangle. Press.

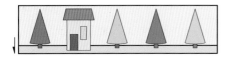

Make 1 row,
3½" × 13½".

Assembling the Quilt

1 Sew six red print 1" squares and five white 1" × 2½" rectangles together to make a sashing row. Make five rows that measure 1" × 13½", including the seam allowances.

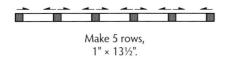

Make 5 rows,
1" × 13½".

2 Sew five blocks and six white 1" × 2½" rectangles together to make a block row. Make four rows that measure 2½" × 13½", including the seam allowances.

Make 4 rows,
2½" × 13½".

3 Arrange the appliquéd row, sashing rows, and block rows as shown in the quilt assembly diagram below. Sew the rows together to make the quilt-top center, which should measure 13½" × 14", including the seam allowances.

4 Sew the white 1½" × 14" strips to opposite sides of the quilt top.

5 Sew a red 1½" square to each end of the white 1½" × 13½" strips. Sew the strips to the top and bottom of the quilt. The quilt top should measure 15½" × 16".

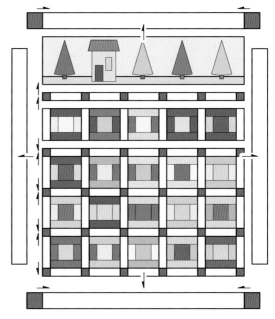

Quilt assembly

Finishing the Quilt

For more details on quilting and finishing, go to
ShopMartingale.com/HowtoQuilt.

1 Layer the backing, batting, and quilt top; baste the
layers together. Hand or machine quilt. The quilt
shown is machine quilted in the ditch of the blocks
and sashing, around the appliqués, and with loops in
the borders.

2 Using the red striped 2¼"-wide strips, make the
binding and attach it to the quilt.

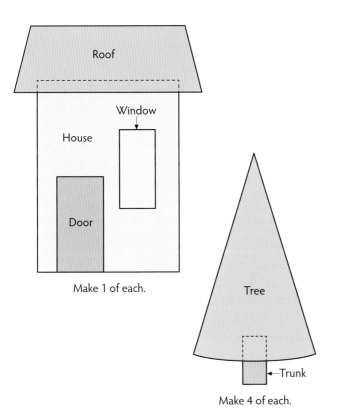

Make 1 of each.

Make 4 of each.

Works like a charm

from **ANNE SUTTON**

It's going to be a jolly holiday filled with sweet dreams
and mini-charm packs if Anne Sutton of Bunny Hill
Designs (BunnyHillDesigns.com) gets to decide what's
under the tree this year.

If I could invent a new mini-charm pack of something
besides fabric, I'd make one out of 2½" squares of
cinnamon sugar pita chips.

Here's a little something I try to remember when I sit
down to sew: Make sure there are pins, scissors, an iron,
and an ironing pad close by.

If I'm not sewing from my own collection of fabrics,
the designer group I'd most likely be working with is
Three Sisters.

When it comes to basics, I love Bella Solids. I have a
closetful!

On a day when I can only squeeze in a little time to
quilt, I'll most likely spend it stitching appliqué.

Lots of good things come in mini size! Besides mini-
charm squares, I like Mini Coopers. We have a bright
red one.

If I'm settled in for sewing and need a good binge-
watching show in the background, I'll turn on *House
of Cards* or *Grey's Anatomy.*

If I had to name a color that every quilt could use a
dash of, it'd be pink, of course!

Leftover charms, if there are any, most likely end up
in my bag with squares to be made into hexies.

Tulip Time by Pat Sloan

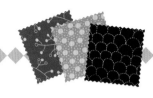

- **FINISHED SIZE: 32¾" × 32¾"**
- **FINISHED BLOCK: 8" × 8"**
- **MINI-CHARM PACKS NEEDED:** ■ ■ ■

Piece mini-charms together to create patchwork fabric for cutting into posies. Then fusible appliqué makes quick work of this springtime wall hanging.

Materials

Yardage is based on 42"-wide fabric. Mini-charm squares are 2½" × 2½".

3 mini-charm packs of assorted prints for blocks
(you'll need 14 red, 16 green, 4 gray, and 76 assorted squares)
1 yard of white print for background
⅓ yard of red print for binding
1⅛ yards of fabric for backing
37" × 37" piece of batting
⅝ yard of paper-backed fusible web
30" length of ⅛"-wide green rickrack for stems
Appliqué basting glue
Cardstock for templates

Cutting

All measurements include ¼"-wide seam allowances.

From the white print, cut:
2 strips, 2½" × 28¾"
2 strips, 2½" × 32¾"
1 strip, 8½" × 42"; crosscut into 4 squares, 8½" × 8½"
1 square, 12¾" × 12¾"; cut the square into quarters diagonally to yield 4 side triangles
2 squares, 9½" × 9½"; cut the squares in half diagonally to yield 4 corner triangles

Continued on page 86

Continued from page 85

From the red print, cut:
4 strips, 2¼" × 42"

From the fusible web, cut:
1 strip, 4½" × 18½"
1 strip, 4½" × 16½"

Making the Appliqué Blocks

For more detailed instructions on fusible appliqué, go to ShopMartingale.com/HowtoQuilt. Press the seam allowances as indicated by the arrows.

1 Trace the tulip and leaf patterns on page 90 onto cardstock to make templates. Cut out each shape on the traced line.

2 Arrange 14 red and 4 gray squares in two rows of 9 squares each. Sew the squares in each row together. Join the rows to make a 4½" × 18½" pieced strip. Press the 4½" × 18½" strip of fusible web onto the wrong side of the pieced strip.

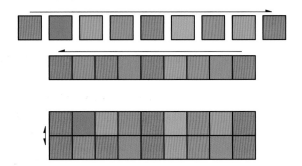

3 Trace the tulip template onto the paper side of the fused strip four times. Try to place the center of each tulip on or near a gray square. Cut out the tulips on the traced lines.

4 Arrange 16 green squares in two rows of eight squares each. Sew the squares in each row together. Join the rows to make a 4½" × 16½" pieced strip. Press the 4½" × 16½" strip of fusible web onto the wrong side of the pieced strip.

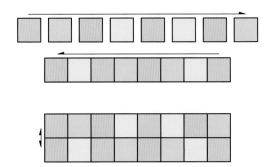

5 Trace the leaf template onto the paper side of the fused green strip eight times. Cut out the leaves on the traced lines.

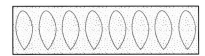

6 Position a tulip on a white 8½" square as shown below. Cut the rickrack into four 7½" lengths. Using basting glue, secure a rickrack stem to the square, tucking the top end under the tulip. Position two leaves on the square. Following the manufacturer's instructions, fuse the tulip and leaves to the square.

7 Stitch the tulip and leaves to the square using a blanket stitch and matching thread. Topstitch through the center of the rickrack using matching thread. Make four tulip blocks that measure 8½" square, including the seam allowances.

Make 4 blocks,
8½" × 8½".

Making the Center Block and Sashing Units

1 Arrange 16 print squares in four rows of four squares each. Sew the squares in each row together. Join the rows to make a block that measures 8½" square, including the seam allowances.

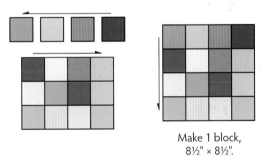

Make 1 block,
8½" × 8½".

2 Sew four print squares together to make a sashing unit. Make 10 units that measure 2½" × 8½", including the seam allowances. Sew six print squares together to make a sashing unit. Make two units that measure 2½" × 12½", including the seam allowances.

Make 10 units,
2½" × 8½".

Make 2 units,
2½" × 12½".

Assembling the Quilt

1 Arrange the tulip blocks, center block, sashing units, and white side and corner triangles as shown in the quilt assembly diagram below. Sew the pieces together into diagonal rows. Join the rows, adding the white corner triangles last. The quilt top should measure 28¾" square, including the seam allowances.

2 The setting triangles were cut a bit oversize for easier cutting and piecing. Trim and square up the quilt top, making sure to leave ¼" beyond the points of all the blocks for seam allowances.

3 Sew the white 2½" × 28¾" strips to opposite sides of the quilt top. Sew the white 2½" × 32¾" strips to the top and bottom of the quilt to complete the border. Press all seam allowances toward the borders. The quilt top should measure 32¾" square.

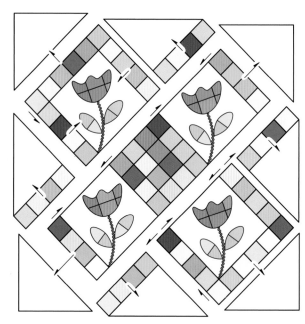

Quilt assembly

Appliquéing the Circles

1 Trace the circle pattern on page 90 onto the paper side of the remaining fusible web eight times. Roughly cut out the circles.

2 Following the manufacturer's instructions, press a fusible-web circle onto the wrong side of each of the remaining eight print squares. Cut out each circle on the line.

3 Remove the paper backing from each circle. Referring to the quilt photo on page 85, arrange and fuse the circles on the setting triangles and press. Check to make sure the appliqués are securely attached, and press again if necessary.

4 Stitch around the circles using a blanket stitch and matching thread.

Finishing the Quilt

For more details on quilting and finishing, go to ShopMartingale.com/HowtoQuilt.

1 Layer the backing, batting, and quilt top; baste the layers together. Hand or machine quilt. The quilt shown is machine quilted with a grid in the center block, straight lines in the sashing, and meandering with loops in the background.

2 Using the red 2¼"-wide strips, make the binding and attach it to the quilt.

Works like a charm

from PAT SLOAN

Pat Sloan (PatSloan.com) is growing a garden of flowers year-round thanks to her fast and fun fusible-appliqué technique!

This works like a charm for me every time: using my Aurifil thread kits, which match my projects.

I store my mini-charm packs in a vintage sewing-machine drawer. They look so darling all lined up.

If I could invent a new mini-charm pack of something besides fabric, I'd make one out of 2½" squares of TIME. Open, use, and repeat.

Here's a little something I try to remember when I sit down to sew: take my time and enjoy the process.

If I'm not sewing from my own collection of fabrics, the designer groups I'd most likely be working with are Fig Tree and French General.

When it comes to basics, I love Grunge Dots!

On a day when I can only squeeze in a little time to quilt, I'll most likely spend it petting my fabric.

Lots of good things come in mini size! Besides mini-charm squares, I like York Minis Peppermint Patties.

If I had to name a color that every quilt could use a dash of, it'd be polka dots!

Leftover charms, if there are any, most likely end up in my 2½" scrap bin to use as starting units when I make Nine Patch blocks.

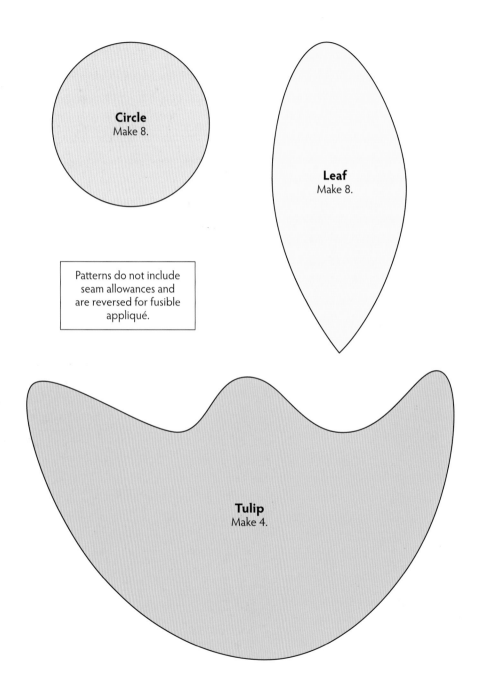

Circle
Make 8.

Leaf
Make 8.

Patterns do not include
seam allowances and
are reversed for fusible
appliqué.

Tulip
Make 4.

Hopscotch Table Runner by Sandy Gervais

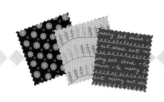

- **FINISHED SIZE:** 16½" × 42½"
- **FINISHED BLOCK:** 13" × 13"
- **MINI-CHARM PACKS NEEDED:** ■■■

Set the table for plenty of compliments with this stunning runner as your centerpiece.

Materials

Yardage is based on 42"-wide fabric. Mini-charm squares are 2½" × 2½".

3 mini-charm packs of assorted prints for blocks
    (you'll need 84 darks and 24 lights)
⅝ yard of cream check for blocks and border
⅓ yard of aqua plaid for binding
1⅜ yards of fabric for backing
21" × 47" piece of batting

Cutting

All measurements include ¼"-wide seam allowances.

From the cream check, cut:

3 strips, 2½" × 42"; crosscut into 48 squares,
    2½" × 2½"
2 strips, 2⅛" × 42"; crosscut into 36 squares,
    2⅛" × 2⅛"
2 strips, 2" × 39½"
2 strips, 2" × 16½"

From the aqua plaid, cut:

4 strips, 2¼" × 42"

Making the Blocks

Press the seam allowances as indicated by the arrows.

1 Choose 12 dark squares. Trim the squares to 2⅛" × 2⅛" and set them aside for step 4.

2 Draw a diagonal line from corner to corner on the wrong side of each cream check 2½" square. Place a marked square on a dark 2½" square, right sides together. Sew ¼" from both sides of the drawn line. Cut on the line to yield two half-square-triangle units. The units should measure 2⅛" square, including the seam allowances. Make 96 cream check half-square-triangle units.

Make 96 units,
2⅛" × 2⅛".

3 Repeat step 2, using the light 2½" squares and 24 dark squares to make 48 half-square-triangle units that measure 2⅛" square, including the seam allowances.

Make 48 units,
2⅛" × 2⅛".

4 Lay out 32 cream check half-square-triangle units, 16 light half-square-triangle units, four dark 2⅛" squares, and 12 cream check 2⅛" squares in eight rows as shown. Sew the pieces in each row together. Join the rows to make a block. Make three blocks that measure 13½" square, including the seam allowances.

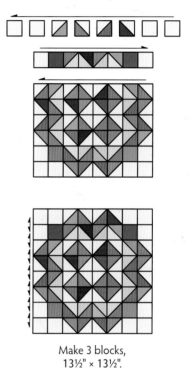

Make 3 blocks,
13½" × 13½".

Assembling the Table Runner

1 Join the blocks to make a row that measures 13½" × 39½", including the seam allowances.

2 Sew the cream check 2" × 39½" strips to the long edges of the table runner. Sew the cream check

Works like a charm

from **SANDY GERVAIS**

Sandy Gervais (PiecesfromMyHeart.net) serves up a heaping helping of mini-charm fun with her latest fabric and pattern designs.

This tool works like a charm for me every time: a Clover needle threader.

I store my mini-charm packs on a shelf stacked by holiday/theme.

If I could invent a new mini-charm pack of something besides fabric, I'd make one out of 2½" squares of sunshine for the long gray winters we have in Iowa.

Here's a little something I try to remember when I sit down to sew: done is better than absolute perfection.

When it comes to basics, I love something with a printed texture rather than a complete solid.

On a day when I can only squeeze in a little time to quilt, I'll most likely spend it playing with color combinations.

Lots of good things come in mini size! Besides mini-charm squares, I like Mini Boden—adorable clothes for the grand kiddos.

If I'm settled in for sewing and need a good binge-watching show in the background, I'll turn on *Sex and the City*.

If I had to name a color that every quilt could use a dash of, it'd be warm red.

2" × 16½" strips to the short ends of the runner. The table runner should measure 16½" × 42½".

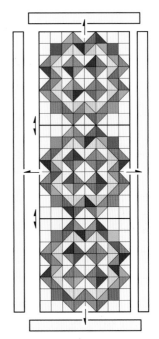

Table-runner assembly

Finishing the Table Runner

For more details on quilting and finishing, go to ShopMartingale.com/HowtoQuilt.

1 Layer the backing, batting, and table runner; baste the layers together. Hand or machine quilt. The table runner shown was machine quilted in an allover pattern by Karen M. Burns.

2 Using the aqua 2¼"-wide strips, make the binding and attach it to the quilt.

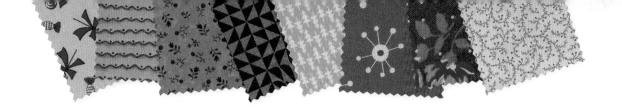

Meet the Contributors

Lisa Bongean
LisaBongean.com

Lynne Hagmeier
KTQuilts.com

Brenda Riddle
AcornQuiltandGiftCompany.com

Betsy Chutchian
BetsysBestQuiltsandMore.blogspot.com

Brigitte Heitland
BrigitteHeitland.de

Kathy Schmitz
KathySchmitz.com

Karla Eisenach
TheSweetwaterCo.com

Stacy Iest Hsu
etsy.com/market/Stacy_Iest_Hsu

Laurie Simpson
MinickandSimpson.blogspot.com

Sandy Gervais
PiecesfromMyHeart.net

Jen Kingwell
JenKingwellDesigns.blogspot.com

Pat Sloan
PatSloan.com

**Barbara Groves and
Mary Jacobson**
MeandMySisterDesigns.com

Sandy Klop
AmericanJane.com

Anne Sutton
BunnyHillDesigns.com

Jo Morton
JoMortonQuilts.com

Corey Yoder
CorianderQuilts.com

Discover more fabulous quilt patterns
by your favorite Moda designers

Explore all the inspiring books in the "Moda All-Stars" series, where you'll discover fresh takes on classic blocks, innovative how-to tips, and clever settings that will make the fabric you love shine. Try a different technique, learn a new sewing trick, and get inspired to make a beautiful quilt today!

Find them all at your local quilt shop or online at ShopMartingale.com

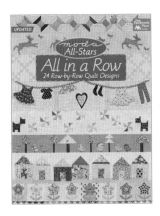